The Alphabet of the Traveler

# THE ALPHABET
## OF THE TRAVELER

*Corrado Paina*

**Mansfield** Press

*To the long nights with Macho, Erio, Chicco, Vanni, Flaviano, Cioffa, and Luigi.*

Library and Archives Canada Cataloguing in Publication

Paina, Corrado, 1954-
    The alphabet of the traveler / Corrado Paina.

Poems.
ISBN 1-894469-25-9

    1. Travel--Poetry.  I. Title.

PS8581.A484A64 2006      C811'.6    C2006-902246-1

Design: Mansfield Creative
Cover Photo: iStockphoto

The publication of *The Alphabet of the Traveler*
has been generously supported by
The Canada Council for the Arts and
The Ontario Arts Council.

**Mansfield** Press Inc.
25 Mansfield Avenue, Toronto, Ontario, Canada M6J 2A9
Publisher: Denis De Klerck
www.mansfieldpress.net

The Canada Council   Le Conseil des Arts
for the Arts         du Canada
SINCE 1957           DEPUIS 1957

ONTARIO ARTS COUNCIL
CONSEIL DES ARTS DE L'ONTARIO

FOR LUIGI MATTIAZZI

# TABLE OF CONTENTS

# Prologue

There, all is order and beauty,
Luxury, calm and sensual pleasure.
(*Invitation to a Journey*)
Charles Baudelaire

The diaries of the traveler are like snowflakes. They are destined to melt. They are long and empty glances from the window of the train, of the airplane, from the bridge of the ship. They are the confirmations of spaces and solitudes; they are linguistic rehearsals, exercises to prolong boredom. The traveler we are talking about doesn't count the seas, nor does he want to conquer the mountains. The traveler has weak arms and maybe he has a weak soul. He is certainly selfish but he is not bad. Harmless? Not always. The traveler is like a musician. He follows another music. His and nobody else's.

— TORONTO

## Anonymity

The traveler is jealous of his anonymity, but the traveler cannot be anonymous. In many countries he has more money than the locals, in others he will be seen as a model of social displacement and therefore as an object of desire. The traveler is never called by name, sometimes people call him by the colour of his hair, or by the colour of his suit, or by the country where they think he is from (sic!). His name is brought to mind when he checks in at the hotel or when he shows his passport. If the traveler has a proper burial, (but the traveler wants to be cremated), that will be the only time that his name will stand still on this earth.

— TORONTO

# Arthur

Arthur is sitting on a bench or maybe an armchair. His posture reminiscent of his beauty and of his laziness. He could be in front of the sea, or almost certainly in front of a sea of sand. We don't know. His clothing is faded white. A little coat and a pair of bloodless trousers show a proud almost exhibitionistic combination of the civil and the warlike. Both are remains of impossible explorations and fake wars, of phony prayers, of visions. His neck is long and nervous, that sternoclideo mastoid muscle is not that of the disciplined soldier. It is the neck of someone who shows a flash of bravery and in fearful moments, cowardliness. His shaved skull tells us much more; the infantile shape in perpetual development, oblong and capricious, the feminine nape submitting to the neck. There is kindness, there is a straight line in his body which looks like the track of a superior rigor that humans cannot understand. Those who see his eyes will compare them to the empty plates of a scale. The leaned arm raises the opposite shoulder until it is almost sloping. His humerus is not that of a warrior but of a proteiform god. His hanging hand is shameless and without morals. He is ready for the human fatigue. For the animal curiosity. His nails circumcised by the infantile bite. Arthur stands up slowly and he doesn't turn. In his right hand a cane appears. Its ticking will follow him like the fish follows the steamship.

The traveler doesn't read much poetry but he likes to write it. That's because many many years ago he read "The Drunken Boat" and he thought that everything that could be written had already been written. The traveler thinks that Arthur Rimbaud is the traveler par excellence, unconsciously forgetful of the moors of life. He is walking for a few meters in a straight line and he stops and he stares at something. We don't know if a caravan, a ship or a carriage will arrive. He doesn't know either.

— TORONTO

## Bag

The traveler needs a shoulder bag. Without a handle. His suitcase must have a handle. The traveler can also use a trunk. The trunk will be shipped from the last place the traveler stayed. A traveler doesn't carry a backpack. It is a demeaning tool for someone who is neither a boy scout, nor a mountain climber, nor an explorer. The traveler keeps the following items in the bag:

1 razor
shaving soap
toilette soap
shampoo
cologne
1 notebook (bigger than a moleskin)
1 sketchbook
1 box of charcoals and pencils
1 box of notepaper and envelopes
1 or 2 books
several pens

The traveler doesn't usually carry a camera.
He prefers to draw and mail the drawings to himself. As in the novel by Perec. The traveler is like a hermit crab. He carries his house on his shoulders.

— FROM THE BALCONY IN VIA ANGERA, MILANO

**Being**

Why does the traveler travel? There is something that breaks the straight line and lures him. A name, a river, a point. The traveler is also a traveler of human beings. He crosses their bodies and souls.

— VIGEVANO, PALAZZO DUCALE

## Boats

Even the traveler smiles at the boats, and he smiles as well at the metaphors. The traveler uses the train, the ship, the airplane, as means of transportation. The traveler doesn't like to drive, he likes to be driven around. He chooses a place, but not the course. He is not a helmsman. A deviation doesn't bother him. The traveler doesn't follow any course.

— MONFALCONE

## Books

The books are not the offspring of the same parent and they are not brothers. Not only are they different but they have also been begotten differently. Therefore the traveler doesn't read following a path, or a particular author, or a blood relationship. He reads what he finds around. The book is not only about words, it is above all an object. There are books on which the traveler likes to write, in the blank spaces, over the printed lines and on the flaps. There are books, which appear miraculously, like rabbits from a hat, books that find a nest in the hands, books that don't tremble when the train quivers and climbs. Thus, the traveler reads Lautreamont and drops it out of boredom, because of urgency, because of the impossibility. The books of il Pulcino e l'Elefante by Casiraghy cannot be neglected and the traveler keeps them inside a bigger book which, when opened, could contain a smaller book and a smaller one and so on...
The traveler doesn't want to renew the pleasure of reading the familiar writer and leaves the book on a bench, on a table of a coffee bar, on the seat of a cab, in a streetcar. With no regret.

— OSNAGO

## Cities

Cities change and it could also be said that they never change. We change and consequently they do. It's a good relationship to have with cities. Less conjugal. It is like losing memory each time and not being afraid. Because there is nothing to remember. It is all new, all to be discovered. The traveler should not have any memory.

– MILANO

## Classic

It is during another stop that Egyptian statues are lined up for a transfer to the Arena. The traveler is consumed by the memory of the father who took his hand and brought him to the opera. It was respectful to dress up for the occasion, to wear the vest and the patent shoes too long and already too tight by the next opera. And the waiting, the bow tie, were becoming familiar like the caffelatte in the morning. But this is somebody else's past, not the traveler's. And the anguish is due to the missed chance. *The Flavii reached their maximum splendor in the First Century D.C.* So says the guide. The traveler doesn't see the guide, doesn't listen to the guide, because he is his own guide, not guiding himself. The traveler doesn't think about the family, about the consequences of the assumption to life, about the queues at the stores, about the original polyptic. The place is always new. The traveler doesn't go where he has already been. He doesn't go where a remembrance, a fresco, a flavor call him. The unknown, the unknowable, the unlearnable are benign gods of the traveler. His comet.

— VERONA, THE SANTA GIULIA

## Clouds

The clouds are not like the traveler. The use of the plural implies there is a group and the traveler always travels alone. The single cloud is not like the traveler either. The traveler is not pushed by the wind, he moves alone. It is his choice. The mood of the traveler is less visible than the mood of the clouds. Too many variables affect the clouds and their features. The traveler also travels when he is trying to settle in. His face is not particularly enlightened by the joyous sun or saddened by the angry storm. But the clouds lure the traveler who watches them and perhaps dreams to travel through them, to find out what is inside them. A cloudless sky is for the traveler like a treeless boulevard, a pigeonless and monumentless square. The clouds are improperly thought of as travelers; they don't know the meaning of freedom.

— MILANO, FIERA DI MILANO

## Complicity

Was the traveler in the painting? Maybe the traveler was Attila? The traveler is not a murderer. He is the accessory to all murders because he has the nature of an accomplice. He looks and proceeds. Therefore he is not Attila. The traveler is not St. Orsola either. St. Orsola was traveling for a reason and the traveler has no objectives. Neither mundane, nor religious. Another personage in the painting is supposed to be Caravaggio. Was Caravaggio a traveler? Yes but he was mainly an artist. The traveler is not an artist. Maybe the traveler is the fourth person in the painting: the man who is trying to stop the arrow? If he did that he would have subverted his inner need to not be involved. The traveler is neutral but he also has feelings. He can be shocked by an event and for this reason the fourth character of the painting of the martyrdom of S. Orsola by Caravaggio could be a traveler, *the* traveler. The traveler goes through history trying to change its course. He changed throughout his itinerary to everywhere. His outstretched hand attests to the fact. There is no salvation. Life runs away. The traveler knows it. He has always known it.

— MILANO — PINACOTECA AMBROSIANA

## Delay

The traveler is never late. A delay doesn't bother him; he has no scheduled appointments, no meetings, no engagements. In the dictionary of the traveler the word delay doesn't exist, it is called extension.

– HOLGUÍN

## Economy

The traveler doesn't have money but he travels most of the time in places where his currency still holds some value. His income comes from a small inheritance. The traveler is profoundly in debt to his father who was the opposite of him. That's why his father has left him some money. The traveler will not leave any money to anybody. Right now he is traveling with the money that came from the sale of his mother's house. It is not a lot of money, but it is a lot for the traveler. He is not, though many would disagree, a parasite. The traveler doesn't ask for much. He buys his own cigarettes, he pays for the hotel, for his food and for his transportation. He could actually be deemed a benefactor to society, because he makes the capital flow in an autarchic way and this contributes to the economy. To all economies.

– HOLGUÍN

# Film

A film is the closest thing to a journey; a film like a journey keeps rolling. But the film is always the same. The traveler is not fond of movies or photography. If the camera shot what the traveler sees without interruption, it could shoot until the death of the traveler. And where would a camera be placed? On the shoulders of the traveler? The traveler is not an archivist and memory is fallacious. Furthermore the traveler never stops traveling even when he dies. He has gone on some of the most beautiful journeys contemplating the ceiling, which is not a metaphor of transportation. Nor is it an allegory of transit.

— TORINO

## Friendship

The traveler doesn't love, he is friendly. The traveler believes in friendship. He is not a revolutionary. He is revolutionized. He goes through the revolution and he never gets out of it, because the journey is a continuous passing through. Friendship is not revolution. Love is revolution. For this reason the traveler doesn't love. Perhaps because he has been loved. Or because he has not been loved. Or maybe, because he doesn't know love. His relationship with himself is also founded on friendship instead of love. The relationship with himself is not made of passions and abandonments as in love matters. Curiosity can be routine. Therefore there is no consumption as in love, there is no decadence in the traveler.

— INTROBIO, REMEMBERING AN ESSAY ON THE ARTS BY TROTSKY

## Geography

Geography and anthropology. Religion, math, comics. And poetry. They are like flowers that the traveler picks in several corners of the earth, in coffee bars, at the post offices, in the railways stations, at the airports, in the temples, in the spaces, in the unspaces, in the emptiness. In the background of ceruse, in the philosophical wool, in the clouds.

— MILANO

# Hotel

Before his arrival the traveler dreams of lingering before opening the door of his room. The desk, the window, the bed and ah! the bathroom are the cardinal points, the corners of the world, the diminutive immanence. Only the traveler knows what fear and ecstasies match the sight of a writing desk which is shelter, barricade and bench in front of a window where he listens to the sound of the rain hitting the glass. He looks at the lightening of the merciless afternoon, which escapes the imperturbable venetians. And it is in front of the window which weakly reflects his curious eyes, his timid skin, that the traveler stops the time, awakens his memory, ordering it to bring him life and passions, lights and actions. Then full and drunk with reminiscences he lays on the bed and he starts a new trip to the meadow at the periphery of the city, to the dune, to the sea carpet... the traveler lies mute and stuffed with formulas of light and blood, silence and emptiness. Who is luckier than the traveler who doesn't know school, college or academy and to the fallen raises universal prayers, and whose world, rectangle or sphere, doesn't swallow into category?

— MILANO, BRESCIA, BERGAMO, TORINO, VERONA

## Individual

It is only the traveler. There are many travelers. The traveler is not alone. It is only the traveler.

— MILANO

## Journey

The traveler doesn't know why he travels. His passion could have started one morning many years ago when he went for a weekend in the country and he hated it. Father and mother woke him up early for fear of being caught in the traffic, and all the family was crammed in a small car for hours while his sisters sang endlessly on the road. Time was not his. So the journey for the traveler is an escape from his childhood memories. He believes that he cannot go against time so he lets time transport him.

— CUBA

## Keys

The key of the traveler's hotel changes every day according to the place where the traveler is. He loves the sound of the key at work. To the traveler the discovery of the hotel room is as exciting as the discovery of a new land. Travel is the key to the new world.

– HOLGUÍN

## Leaves/Seasons

When the traveler is able to avoid the passage of the seasons and to reach places where the leaves are still green, the traveler asks himself if he will ever die. Everybody can be infantile.

– HOLGUÍN

## Map

The traveler doesn't read (almost ever) the map of the country where he is traveling. He prefers to read the maps of other countries because he is not interested in borders. He is not interested in the customs or in the history of the countries. To him they are like strait jackets on the unknown. Only the names and the sound lure his childish restlessness. To him the world is utterly beautiful in its inconsistency.

— HOLGUÍN

## Mother

The mother of the traveler doesn't travel. She never traveled. She didn't like to travel. The traveler doesn't visit her often. The traveler must follow the journey and its rules. His mother knows and waits for a letter from him. Time passes and his mother dies. The traveler keeps writing her. In a strange city, with many celebrations and scarce humanity, the traveler receives a letter from the Mayor of his hometown stating that his mother has passed away. The traveler will never return to his hometown, but he will borrow his mother eyes to see the shining falls and the whimsical sea and the sun peeping between the cracks of the palm leaves. The traveler will recognize his mother's hands in those of a librarian recommending a memoir of Gide's stay in Biskra. The traveler will warm up at the smile borrowed from his mother by a woman taking the bus. It is at sunset that the traveler hears her voice, carried by the waves, maybe by a summer breeze. It is during that hour that the traveler stops, it is during that hour that time stops, it is during that hour that he becomes the son again and he needs her.

— MILANO

## Morality

The traveler is not amoral. Certainly he is not immoral. The traveler is part of things or, better to say, is closer to the exterior of things than the interior of human beings. The traveler is on the outside of human beings.

— MILANO

## Nap

The traveler loves to take a nap after lunch. In some countries he will close his eyes together with a nation fading into unconsciousness. That hour of demi-death will spread all over the city – the countryside up to the sea. The engines will all be shut down. One can hear the far cry of a child and the intermittent obtuse barking of stray dogs. The afternoon in a hotel room looking at the fan, softly sweating while descending into sleep is priceless. Sometimes the awakenings can be traumatic, but the traveler's opinion about this matter must be searched in another page.

– HOLGUÍN

## Notebook

But why does the traveler write? For how long and about what? His words are roads, alleys, routes and maps that are comprehensible only to him. There are interruptions, hurdles, ambushes, mishaps, waitings. The traveler has a lot of time and takes note of everything. The traveler also writes travel poems. They are neither love poems nor civil poems. They are not religious poems. They are scales that only a coalition of ears could hear and understand. The notebook appears and disappears within the hands of the traveler like a rabbit in a hat. It is an illusion, but it has a beating heart.

— MILANO

## Old Age

The traveler ages but he is not aware of it and he will die at a point on the globe. Before dying he will try to gather his strength and try to stand up from the bed. He will fall heavily and he will feel like a boat at the mercy of the waves. It is not the first time that he feels this sensation... and it is not so scary. He can finally contemplate, for the few moments allowed to him, the meaning of jurisdiction.

— MILANO

## Property

Property is not theft. Property doesn't exist. Because nothing cannot own. The traveler doesn't belong. The traveler doesn't own. He is in transit. Even the objects that he is fond of are objects that nobody wants. A razor, a pencil, a knife. They are necessary and they should not be bartered for other objects. If there is property, it is transitory and it has the physiognomy of barter. Sometimes one must abide. But without a stamp of exclusivity. A dawn belongs to everybody. A train tickets expires. Money is spent. And money slips away through the fingers like water. One drinks and property is dissolved. Villa Este, Villa Erba, Villa... unstrung like sanctuaries of an adored god. They are relics, corpses. They are Dubuffet simulacra. The water they lay upon, will outlive people; it will live longer than the bricks. Water is velocity, bricks are the brakes. And the traveler must continue.

— LAKE COMO

## Quest

If there is a quest the traveler doesn't know about it. He has not been informed. He is not aware. The traveler could be considered a shallow man and time is shallow. Life is shallow. The end is shallow. The traveler writes these lines and feels he is shallow. He is also sure that if he falls asleep by tomorrow he will be writing about something else.

– HOLGUÍN

# Remembrance

There is a voice that comes back sometimes. It is his call for help. His father and his mother brought the family to the mountain and they were all having a picnic on the slopes, on a meadow as soft as a cheek where the most beautiful flowers were spread like freckles. A small lake was washing the banks of the meadow. The traveler, who at the time was ten years old, decided to pick some flowers for his mother. He left the tablecloth laid over the thin grass blades and approached the water where the grass was more untidy. There, there were flowers more yellow, larger, where the earth was softening in wet clay. His hands lowered to pick a yellow flower, the tallest of all and he saw the sinuous body of a water snake. It looked huge to him, brown like a giant worm and the child ran away screaming and crying. He called his parents and ran until he found shelter between his mother's arms while his father approached the bank of the small lake with a stick. His parents' sweet voices come back sometimes. The traveler stops his journey to let the remembrance envelope him. His body and his soul are not on a material journey. Fear comes in. For the traveler the future is empty of worries. Even when the traveler stops his journey, the present is still traveling.

– MILANO

## Saturday

In front of an overcrowded renaissance structure, the traveler is try-
ing to glimpse the images surfacing from faded frescos. Sitting on a
bench of a public garden he stares at the church on a sunny afternoon.
Seniors walk trembling, helped by Filipino attendants. A newcomer
seeks shelter from the sun and falls asleep on a bench. A dog breaks
the silence with a lazy bark. The traveler doesn't know if he wants to
go inside the church and he falls asleep too. When the afternoon ends
the sparrows begin their songs. By the end of that afternoon, a
Saturday afternoon, the traveler will get ready for the evening. A trav-
eler must have strong legs and a strong stomach and a mind that does-
n't vacillate at the advance of solitude. Because on a Saturday night
everybody wants to do something. Everybody loves the feeling of
being part of a group. The traveler is human and follows rationally
inevitable patterns. And irrationally he chooses them. It's the time,
the hour of memories, of friends, of faces met somewhere, of over-
heard stories, stored all together in his bag. The traveler cannot kill
time, he must cross it. The traveler is no murderer. The traveler is the
accomplice of boredom, of solitude. That's why he stands up and
starts walking, not knowing where he is heading, and not without see-
ing the Filipino attendants for the last time, walking slowly and hold-
ing in their shining arms the old people with the faded sight. To die
with certainty, before becoming too old, dying like the drunken
ambassador murdered by drunken thugs and thrown in a ditch. Like
the homeless beaten to death. To die with certainty. Maybe on an air-
plane, maybe closing his eyes forever over a novel borrowed from the
reception desk of a hotel. What language does the traveler speak?
None. For he is a great listener. Because the traveler doesn't ever
understand completely. Because he must add some patches to the suit
of life. The beauty of Saturday night shines with youth, shyness,
hunger and anger. They are the beauty marks of Saturday. Did the
traveler ever sit on beauty's knees? He cannot.

He cannot ask questions, he cannot lose himself in her eyes. The youngsters pass by the old church. Who says that they live without caring for monuments? They live in them. The gates of the public garden are going to be closed and the traveler, like all travelers, must decide his direction. It is more difficult to decide what to do in a city than to choose the route to the Indies.

– S. MARIA DELLA FONTANA, MILANO

## Sex

The traveler is like an angel; he has no sex. And he doesn't like certain duties. He doesn't like to announce or to forbid. Sometimes he leaves a scent of jasmine of the Ionic coast and a snowdrop from Valsassina. The traveler loves sex, as much as he loves the clouds. The traveler follows the shadow of sex.

— S. MARIA DELLA FONTANA, MILANO

## Sironi

These gigantic women with that glance lost in the emptiness, with that prebyopia of the great role of mater, warrior and philosopher, cannot be anything else than relics of a dictatorial past. These gigantic canvases disorient the traveler, envelop him in a cloud of socialist realism and urgency of the masses, forcing him to moor in his past for a few moments. The traveler's mother was never like the women of the exhibition, her glance was full of awareness of natural love and empty of historical engagement, and for a moment, only for a moment, he travels back to his roots. It's because of the discipline transfused by these muscular mothers. And the traveler is not foreign to discipline. He simply crossed it, passed it. What is the state for the traveler? For the traveler the state is the border, a stamp. Once all borders, all stamps do not exist anymore, the traveler won't exist anymore. Boris Vian said that the point is not that everybody must be happy, but that each one must be happy. Sironi celebrated the work, which cannot be associated with the journey. Travelling is more of a craft; if travelling and work have something in common, it is discipline.

— TRIENNALE, MILANO

45

## Suit

The traveler has a preference for the colour white. Never for pastel colours. The western traveler associates white with the romantic idea of purity covered with mud. But why the suit? Why not just the pants and a white and blue striped shirt with a little collar or without. In particular areas where the temperature is very high the traveler will wear espadrilles or desert boots. Sandals too (in leather), and never with socks. He will never use clogs. The white suit, or brown in colder seasons, has some precise functions. The coat must have wide pockets, which replace the traveling bag that the traveler uses when he is traveling. In a small pocket of his coat the traveler keeps his lighter (matches are also recommended) for a cigarette he will smoke when he stops in front of the ruins of a temple at the intermission of a journey. He must smoke while he enjoys the tropical breeze in a bus station. The traveler is always ready for any occasion, and as they used to say, before death one must always be ready.
The suit is mandatory.

— MILANO

## Trade

The traveler likes to wonder about people's trades. It is the traveler's game when he watches and/or meets people just once in a lifetime. It is a way of judging people, but it is only an innocent device. The traveler is aware of always being mistaken, but the traveler must still make his own routes; he draws some points, which are signage, that help him to understand somebody else's life. The traveler is a little bit of an architect, a little bit of an urbanist, and a little bit of a plastic surgeon. The traveler does to the others what he doesn't want to be done to himself.

– MILANO

47

## Trattoria

In a trattoria the traveler sits under a pergola and orders something to eat. It has been a few days since he stopped in a city that is proud of its popular eateries. The traveler goes every day to this trattoria, perhaps the last survivor of a splendid generation. The traveler hopes that nothing will change. He will keep going to the same inn until he leaves. He will sit at the same table and he will take a notebook and a book from his bag and he will write and read and eat. He will drink and he will digest. Right after he will smoke. The traveler hopes that no Dorian Grey will enter pompously, noisily, in fancy dress, with a phalanx of friends. The traveler loves to see normal people eating in a trattoria because the food is simple and affordable. And the wine helps him to wonder and to wander. The traveler has always been a little bit selfish and misanthropic. The traveler is also a little bit reactionary.

— MILANO

## Two

Two is a number unrecognized by the traveler. The traveler travels alone. He lives alone. The traveler is not thesis, is not antithesis, he has no identity. The traveler is one.

– MILANO

## Umbabene

ROBERTSON: How about Umbabene?
I bet you have never been to Umbabene?
Terrible place... or to Pernambuco?

LOCKE: No.

ROBERTSON: Airports, taxis, hotels...
they are all the same in the end.

LOCKE: I don't agree. It's us who remain the same.
We translate every situation, every experience,
into the same old codes... we condition ourselves.

ROBERTSON: We are creatures of habit. That's what you mean.

– *The Passenger,* MICHELANGELO ANTONIONI / MARK PEPLOE

## Vanity

In the beginning was the word. And for the traveler nothing has changed. This is not vanity. Perhaps some affectation but definitely not vanity. There is a link with the beginning. To travel, what does it mean? It means to lose oneself, to abandon your features, to destroy friendly physiognomies, to not recognize yourself in the mirror, to not belong. But it is not as complicated as it sounds. In the beginning everything was new. The traveler knows that he can be rejected but the only thing that matters is to continue. Not only ahead, not only upward, not only downward, but to continue. At the cost of falling, falling down. As in the beginning. The traveler is not vain, he is arrogant.

— MILANO

## Watch

The traveler owns a watch. Somebody gave it to him and he looks at it as a necessary object. Maybe he values it as an item for barter. He places the watch in his bag or in his pocket. Instead the traveler uses a sort of mental hourglass, which reminds him of the possibilities of time. The generosity and the narrowness. But the traveler goes against time. His movements are anticlockwise.

— MILANO

## Wine

The traveler drinks his wine with a little bit of anguish. Because it is the only moment that he can show his unknown face to himself and to others. The stories that the traveler tells are not completely truthful.

— MILANO

## Work

What is better? To work from the time one is twenty-five years old to the age of fifty or from when one is fifty years old to seventy? Anyone would be able to use arguments and plausible convictions but the traveler doesn't table such matters. The traveler doesn't work. He knows how to do everything because like the poet he has had a thousand jobs. And like the poet he does everything badly. Like the poet he has been in the hands and in the soul of the world. And he keeps living in it. He is not lazy. He believes that work is the root of all vice.

— MARKET IN PIAZZA LAGOSTA, MILANO

## Writers

The traveler writes but he doesn't want to leave a mark. Or a legacy. Sometimes he writes a journal, sometimes portraits of people (like his drawings), sometimes thoughts – special meditations dictated more by the traveler's tiredness than by a necessity to share. In fact he would like to write things that don't last on the page. The traveler reads an inscription of famous statements on a cippus. On postcards. On a frontispiece. On memorial stones. On the bookstore windows. They have been taken from novels, from collections of poetry. They are bits of thought from writers born in these towns where nobody remembers. Where wars and civil conflicts have moved men and history. In the face of the inhabitants he cannot see love or violent stories – there is no legend, there is no myth. Maybe because the myth and the legend have aged and they should never age. The young will share the confusion, the melancholy, but they don't have any memory. Like the traveler who reads these sentences and doesn't remember any. The surrounding nature has more to say, and prefers showing a fluid body unashamed of cellulitis and crooked bones. Behind that wall of leaves and hills perhaps memories and secrets are hidden and one can feel the silent cries lining up, the quivers, the orgasms. The traveler doesn't want to know more and he will leave. He likes nothing better than the regret of having uncovered the truth.

– ALBA, S. STEFANO BELBO

## Xanadu

The traveler doesn't like the whole idea surrounding Xanadu. He doesn't like the literary, the aesthetic concept of Xanadu. The traveler is not religious. But he is a lay person (because he is a creature of the past) and he believes intimately that there is a Xanadu and that everybody is looking for his or her own Xanadu. The traveler doesn't believe that his Xanadu is better than anybody else's Xanadu. But the traveler is a worldly man and he surrenders to any temptation.

– HOLGUÍN

## Yoke

People's yokes have always been visible to the traveler. His yoke, pre-posterously, is not visible to people. The traveler knows that his life is enviable and he honestly doesn't envy people's lives. He also recognizes that they only think that they envy him, but they really don't want to be in his shoes. What they want is a life with no yoke and that is a life without death. The traveler has no destination, but the final destination will settle him too.

– HOLGUÍN

## Zoo

It is not unusual that the traveler likes cemeteries but it is odd that the traveler likes the zoo. The cemeteries calm him down and inform him about rules and regulations of the journey. But the zoo is full of animals in captivity and freedom is dear to the traveler. He has seen some of these animals living free in the far places of the world. He has seen the illustrations of others in school books. But there are many things about the traveler that are not easy to understand and this is one of them.

— MILANO

## Postscript : The end

The traveler died some time ago on a cargo ship from Lima to Savona. In those days a famous Italian writer also died, killed they say, by a prostitute on a squalid road near the capital. There are expert guides, skilled reporters, brave explorers, curious passengers, ruthless interpreters, unconscious strangers, knowledgeable foreigners, refugees, stowaways, immigrants, migrants and so on...

But the last traveler is dead and nobody misses him. He would not have missed himself either.

— CUBA

Previously published by Corrado Paina:

In Italian:
*Di Corsa*—Mapograph, 1996
*Tempo Rubato*—Atelier 14, 2003
*Darsena Inquinata*—Moderata Durant Editrice, 2005
*Tra Rothko E Tre Finestre*—Ibiskos Editrice, 2006

In English:
*Hoarse Legend*—Mansfield Press, 2000
*The Dowry of Education*—Mansfield Press, 2004

Corrado Paina was born in Milan, Italy in 1954
and he has lived in Toronto, Canada since 1987.
The *Alphabet of the Traveller* is his seventh book.